START YOUR OWN FREE

MAGAZINE TODAY

MAKE MONEY FROM ADVERTS

JOSHUA AONDOAKAA

START YOUR OWN FREE MAGAZINE TODAY!

Published in the USA by Gateway International

Empowerment House

New York

Publishing rights administered on Amazon by Gateway International

For Publisher Enquiries Contact:

Goldenamerica2017@gmail.com

Presented To:

_____

From:

_____

Date:

_____

Sign:

_____

INTRODUCTION

"How can I start my very own community, national or even international magazine?"

IMPORTANT NOTE:

The examples and case studies on starting a magazine in this book are based on actual practical experiment in the UK. However, this process is generic and can be used to start your own magazine anywhere in the world.

The purpose of this book is to help you do exactly that. With help from the pages of this book you will have all the resources and training required to start your own magazine.

Your magazine can feature a wealth of local news, views, information & topical issues of interest to the community and is delivered free or at a minimal price to community households each month or weekly. Each magazine is also published online to provide residents & advertisers ease of access and you, the business owner, further revenues.Local businesses have an opportunity to advertise in the magazine and reach their critical target market of local residents.

"How will I get paid & how much?"

A typical magazine contains 40 pages. Each paid page will

generate an average of£130 income from advertisers. Advertisers should pay you directly before you go to print. The total revenue for a typical magazine is £3,475 from an average of 30 -40 advertisers. Magazines can, of course, grow much larger than 40 pages and generate more income & profits.

The additional revenues you will collect include residual fees, commissions & online advertising fees. All of these are added directly to your magazine revenues to create your overall profit.

Costs will vary dependent on the number of pages & distribution but will normally average c£1470 including printing, distribution*, support* and insurance.

This means your profit from an average magazine averages £2,005 each month excluding additional income.

"Sounds great, but I've never published a magazine before"

That's why I have written this book to help you. All you need to do is add advertisements. The two key skills you will need are a willingness to follow a successful system & a commitment to succeed.

"Why will businesses advertise in my magazine?"

The single most important market for all local businesses is their local community. Your magazine will offer advertisers an opportunity to promote their products or services in a high quality, beautifully presented magazine that is delivered free to local households each month and retained for at least a month due to the local news, views, listings & useful information contained inside.

"My community only has a limited number of businesses located within the community, will these provide me with enough business?"

It's not just the advertisers located in your community that will wish to market to your community but any advertiser regardless of their location who wants to sell their goods & services to your community. This might mean businesses from neighboring villages, towns, cities, regions or even

national based businesses.

Most communities in the UK are serviced by between 900 – 2,900 businesses within 20 miles. To be successful you need to ensure an average of just 40 advertisers each month! Don't forget that the majority of your advertisers will place 3, 6, 9 or 12 month contracts, so any new advertisers each month increase your profits further!

"How do I attract advertisers?"

If you decide, for instance, that you are going to offer 10% off standard advertising rates for customers choosing to purchase a Full Page advert for a 12 month contract you can send it to every prospective advertiser in your database at the click of a button!

As well as meeting with potential advertisers, send prospects a copy of their magazine with a standard letter outlining their offer.

CHAPTER ONE

Sales and Marketing

The Keys to *Success*

Revenue Streams: Online & Offline

There are 5 main revenue streams that will create your overall profit;

1. Traditional magazine advertising   Offline

2. Online advertising adverts   Online

3. Email campaigns   Online

4. SMS campaigns   Online

5. Affiliate marketing   Online

6. Flyer design & distribution   Offline

To consider each in turn:

1. Traditional magazine advertising.

This is your first and most important revenue stream. It might not be the largest but without this advertising your other revenue streams will prove difficult. Your central proposition is the production of a high quality, glossy magazine that is delivered to homes in your chosen community. This, alone, provides you with a competitive advantage as your competitors, if they exist, will be operating a low quality, poorly designed pamphlet. You do, of course, have further significant advantages as your magazine is also published online and this activity will generate you 4 further revenue streams.

2. Online advertising

This is likely to be your second most important

revenue stream and also provides your all-important residual income. Residual income is income you earn for an activity that you carried out once but get paid for repeatedly. A good example is an author who receives a fee for each copy of each book sold. The author wrote the book once but receives income each time someone purchases that book.

Your advertisers are placed in your online directory on

your magazine site for a small monthly fee. You carry out the work of placing their advertisement into the directory once and get paid for each month that the advertisement appears.

This residual income builds up over time and provides a significant boost to your bottom line profits.

3. Email campaigns

Email marketing is a fast growing and profitable marketing channel. Many email campaigns are carried out by national & Multi-national companies as a mass market activity. Whilst you will have access to these advertisers through Community Times corporate you are also able to offer your local advertisers a unique service. Your competitions & online magazine site will collect opt-in marketing data from local residents that you are able to use to provide your advertisers

with targeted email campaigns.

Let's use the example of a local ladies fashion shop that has recently started stocking an exclusive range of designer dresses. You could design an email campaign that includes pictures of some of the dresses, the background of the designer and an introductory offer of 10% off any purchase from this range before the end of the month.

The email would then be sent to the email address of every female in your local community marketing database for a fee to the advertiser. Commercial rates for email send vary between £150 - £200/thousand emails.

Community Times licensees commonly collect over a thousand email addresses from their local community which provide a high density of local, opt-in email addresses that local & national companies will be keen to utilize.

4. SMS campaigns

Text messaging has provided mobile phone

companies with an enormous revenue base which they simply hadn't foreseen. Initially used by the youth market, SMS messaging is now firmly established as an important commercial channel in it's own right and offers advertisers a uniquely effective channel.

In exactly the same way that you collect email addresses your competitions & online magazine site will collect opt-in marketing data from local residents that you are able to use to provide your advertisers with targeted SMS campaigns.

Let's use the example of a local restaurant that is launching a weekday "Early Bird" special offer. You can create an SMS campaign that informs local residents of the offer and invites them to come along to the restaurant and get a further 10% off on production of the text message on their mobile phone.

The text messages would then be sent to the mobile phones of every person in your local community marketing database for a fee to the advertiser. Commercial rates for

SMS send vary between £0.10 - £0.20 per message. You are able to purchase SMS credits within the Business System.

Community Times licensees commonly collect over a thousand mobile numbers from their local community which provide a high density of local, opt-in mobile numbers that local & national companies will be keen to utilize. 5. Affiliate marketing

Affiliate marketing is now a significant proportion of income derived from the Internet. Affiliate schemes, once set-up, will provide a steady stream of income into your business. The schemes work by selecting & promoting products and services on your online magazine site. The site will be viewed by a significant proportion of your local community and you will receive payment for each person that conducts business after clicking on an affiliate advertisement on

your site.

5. Flyer design & distribution

Your relationship with your printer will enable you to be able to offer flyer design & delivery to your selected customers. A typical cost for this to your advertisers would be:

You will be able to get 5000 flyers designed & produced for c£150 and distribute alongside your magazines at no extra cost. The cost you charge your advertisers is, as always, your decision but a good guideline for design, print & distribution of 5000 flyers would be £375. This provides your advertisers with an excellent incentive to order this service from you as they will be saving £200 (more than 33%) for comparable services. It will also provide you with a healthy profit margin of £225 per flyer campaign.

Pricing is an issue over which you can have as much or as little flexibility as you wish, it's your business! The pitfall to avoid that many new businesses make is to underprice their product or service as they lack confidence in their proposition. The prices we recommend are good, competitive & achievable for the service that you provide to your customers. If you drop your prices without increasing volume you will see your profits fall and if you increase your prices and reduce sales you may also see your profits fall. Conversely, many of our licensees have been able to increase their prices as their customers are very happy with the service they get and the increase in business they receive from advertising in Community Times.

Our advice, when starting out, is to use our example rate card. Once you are established you may well be able to increase your prices and your profitability but you will be able to do this from a position of strength.

Packages

It is standard practice in publishing to offer advertising packages. For your Community Times magazine we recommend making the following packages available to advertisers. Remember that the more packages you sell the more time you will have each month to increase your revenues from new advertisers & additional revenue streams.

Sponsorship

Each month you can offer your readers the chance to win a Grand Prize e.g. 2 tickets to New York. Entrants visit the online magazine site and complete an entry form to enter the competition.An email confirming entry is sent to each entrant on completion of each entry form. At the close of the competition each entrant is emailed the competition results. Sponsorship is available to advertisers to brand & advertise in the following areas:

Online Entry Form: Branded "in association with {Advertisers Name & Logo}"
Email confirmation:Branded "in association with {Advertisers Name & Logo}"+ advertorial copy
Email results: Branded "in association with {Advertisers Name}" + advertorial copy

Cost *I* month: £250 inc. of email design & build.

The big question is, "Should you publish these and make them public knowledge, or should you keep them until asked for a deal?"

The answer will be different for each licensee. It will depend on your advertisers, your chosen community

and your skills & experience. We recommend that for your first edition you do not make these publicly available. If asked, you have the information available but will not risk giving away unnecessary discounts.

Repeat Orders & Residual Income

The keys to running a profitable business that provides you with an excellent income and the time to enjoy it are repeat orders & residual income.

Repeat Orders

Each edition of your magazine will require between 30-40 advertisers purchasing a mixture of ' % & full page advertisements to make it a profitable revenue stream. If you have to constantly replace advertisers in each edition this will require a significant time investment from you.

Perhaps of more consequence is the fact that successful publishing businesses always generate high levels of repeat business and this is a good indicator

that your magazine is providing a valuable service to your customers.

Community Times has been strategically developed to provide licensees with the best possible chance to achieve repeat orders. It is produced as a high quality, glossy magazine to provide advertisers with a brand & product that they are pleased to be associated with. This enables you to sell advertising to companies for whom advertising spend is viewed as an essential investment.
These companies will expect to be able to book long term advertising with you as their advertising spend is part of their short1 medium & long term planning.
You should target a 75% repeat order ratio from your customers. This will ensure that your magazine is profitable before you even begin to sell further advertising for each edition as well as providing you enormous time benefits.
Residual Income

As explained in the Online Marketing section residual income is income paid each month for work that you have carried out just once. Once each online advertisement has been set-up your customers will pay you to remain in your directory listing. Once you have achieved customers for this service you will receive revenue each month even if you decide to carry out no

further work on developing this revenue stream. The online magazine changes each month and offers a variety of competitions, offers & content to attract visitors each month.

You can also use PPC (Pay Per Click)

Advertising to promote the site online to maximize visitors and make the online directory increasingly attractive and beneficial to advertisers.

CHAPTER TWO

Marketing Strategy

Your marketing strategy has to address two separate constituencies:

1. Your local business community

2. Your local community residents

a. **Your local business community**

Local business owners will comprise a substantial proportion of your client base. It is important that you get to know as many decision makers & opinion formers as possible. The best way to do this is to attend business network lunches in your area. At these events you will meet local business owners in a relaxed environment and have an opportunity to introduce your service. The

majority of attendees at such events will be seeking to network with local businesses and build relationships for mutual benefit. Your service is targeted at helping local businesses to increase their sales to their prime market through multiple channels in a unique and cost effective way. Unlike almost everyone else in the room your service will be of potential benefit to everyone!

3. **Your local community residents**

To be truly effective your magazine must provide value & interest to the community.Many recipients of the magazine will retain each edition for reference for many months.

To provide a valuable service and deal with matters of importance to the local community you have to have your finger on the pulse of what's going on in your community.Coffee mornings, W.I meetings and P.T.A.'s are all excellent forums for finding out the issues that are exercising the community.

A small word of caution here as you must take care not to polarize opinions amongst your readers and not use your magazine to promote your personal point of view however strong your convictions.

Sales Process

You will be making sales using many different channels but your first sales method should be to visit local shops & businesses in person. Many people have a perception that this is a difficult process with little return on your time investment. Nothing could be further from the truth. It is by speaking to people, face to face, that you will gain an enormous amount of feedback and understanding of the local circumstances and issues that you need to manage to your advantage. Flyers mailshots, telephone calls, email campaigns & SMS campaigns are all channels that you will be using to grow your business but there is no better way to quickly achieve the understanding and relationships you need than meeting with your prospective clients. We provide you with scripts and a media pack to make this as easy as possible. The first time you walk through the door of a prospective customer and ask for 5 minutes of their time may be hard if you've never done it before but you will be amazed at how quickly your confidence grows and your sales "pitch" develops!

The key to success in sales is to ensure you are

confident, cheerful and bright. Don't try and stick to the suggested scripts word for word, your delivery will come across as "wooden", but adapt them until they feel comfortable for you to say whilst retaining the key messages.

If the owner doesn't have 5 minutes to listen to your sales pitch, try and establish a good time to call back. If they are always too busy to speak leave them with a media pack to review and check that they will be happy to receive a follow up call or visit from you when they've had the opportunity to consider your offer.

Sales Activities:

Your business system ensures that this critical activity is managed efficiently. Even excellent sales people often struggle to follow up effectively. Your business system ensures you convert as many prospects into sales as possible & even more importantly, look after the customers you have to ensure a long & fruitful relationship. This will be the key to your commercial success!

Below are the key activities that you should consider. Whilst all of these are relevant the importance of

Person to Person cannot be overemphasized. This should always be your main focus of activity. Once you get over any initial reticence you will also find it the most enjoyable. You are providing a unique, quality service that provides value to your readers and your advertisers and their positive feedback will be enjoyable!

Person to person:

Dress smartly practice your lines, smile & be confident. That's the hard bit! If you can approach each prospective advertiser in this manner you will fill your magazine in no time. The first time may be difficult but it gets easier and your sense of fulfilment at achieving sales will make you hungry to do it again. Remember to get the contact details of the decision maker if they are not available and follow up!

Telephone calls:

Yellow Pages & Thompson Directories are great resources to find out the contact details of businesses that wish to conduct business in your area. Although you don't have to dress up too smartly to work the telephone you'll be amazed at the difference dressing for business, practicing your lines, smiling and being confident makes on the telephone as well as in person. Again, remember to get the contact details of the decision maker if they are not available and follow up.

Email:

A surprising percentage of local businesses have yet to

utilize email & the Internet effectively. Your business system and proposition to advertisers does just that! Ensure that your emails are concise, spelt correctly, have a clear outcome & look attractive. You will be offering to reach their local community via this medium so it is important that your emails demonstrate these qualities. Follow up your emails with a telephone call.

SMS:

This medium requires you to be concise. A short, succinct message is required. Provide your number in the text and give them a compelling reason to call you. "Last page in local magazine available

Mailshot:

Successful mail shots grab the readers attention instantly. If your recipient has to read the document closely to gain an outline understanding of your proposition it's likely that your campaign will be a failure. If you can grab the readers attention with a compelling headline that outlines a direct benefit to them your campaign will succeed.

Quick start Guide to Selling.

Get your dates right

Getting you first edition up and running is going to be the most time consuming of all your editions. You will need to be aware of your first, planned publication date. All essential dates are available within the CT Business

System.

Having a clear understanding of publishing deadlines is very important for you and your advertisers. They will need to provide you with artwork, copy or other materials by a specified date..

Know your offering

Prepare your Media Pack and become familiar with the rates and the information provided. Make any local modification that you feel may be necessary.

Set your Sales Targets

Aim to have at least 30 - 40 advertisers in you first edition.

Maximize your time efficiency

A key element of success is working out when you are going to best use your time. There will be a number of activities that can only be done during traditional working hours, such as visiting businesses or speaking to decision makers. Make sure you use your time

wisely, if you only have limited time available during business working hours make sure you spend it doing these activities and not with other non-time critical activities, such as letter writing, ad design or production.

Get recognition

There will be a number of businesses in the area that people will recognize and have a strong social and commercial standing in the community/town. Getting one of these on the front cover of your first edition will make selling the rest of space a lot easier. If you can quickly get one of these businesses on the front cover, CT can modify your media flyers to reflect the actual design of the first edition.

CHAPTER THREE

Selling Methods & Tips

1. Door to Door

Actually meeting people face to face is your best and most effective way of getting business. Although most businesses and business owners are often very busy all businesses are looking for new customers to increase their sales. The Community Times magazine offers them a great opportunity to promote their products and services.

Where you have businesses that offer easy access, e.g. High Street retailers it is worthwhile just turning up and asking to speak to the owner/manager.

If you ask for just a few minutes to explain who you are and what you are doing, most people will give you 5 minutes of their valuable time. You have 5 minutes to

get across how beneficial advertising in your Community Times Magazine might be for their business.

Don't expect to sell to everyone in the first 5 minutes.

These 5 minutes are your opportunity to either sell, engage interest, leave information or arrange a convenient time for an appointment.

In many cases advertisers will agree to purchase advertising space there and then due to the high quality & design specification of your magazine.

The main points you need to get across in your 5 minutes are: This is a high quality, low cost and effective advertising channel targeted at home owners in the community.

The magazine is delivered directly through the letterboxes of over 3000 households and another 400 copies are distributed to local communal locations such as waiting rooms, take-aways and local shops.

Unlike many high quality publications the Community Times magazine offers advertising rate from just £40 a

month, which can include design and free inclusion in
the online magazine.

The Community based magazine contains lots of local
interesting community information and articles that
make the magazine useful to the local readership and
something they will keep at home on a monthly basis as
a point of reference.

The Community Times also provides a unique online version of
the magazine. All advertisers are featured in the online version.

The online magazine is available to a wide readership
and features on Google for searches such as <Area>
shops, <Area> restaurants and <Area> Information.

Companies featured on the premium pages may also
have the opportunity to feature in the editorial and in the
monthly newsletter that goes out to all the registered
subscribers to the email newsletter. (Remember you can
also sell extra space here.)

2. Telecalls

This can be a very cost effective way of making sales. Do be aware, however, that the conversion rate is likely to be less than face-to-face. People buy people and being with them will help them buy.

There are 2 approaches you can take to a Telecall.

1. Attempt to make an appointment. Find out who the decision maker is and then arrange to see them.

2. Use this as an opportunity to sell your space. The 5 minute pitch in the section above will get you into a conversation and will lead to either a more involved discussion, a sale or a request for more information.

3. Mailshots

Contacting people by this method is cost effective and time efficient. See the Business System for example letters and ideas.

This method can also be used in conjunction with the above methods. (If you have a name from a visit or a telecall a follow-up letter is always well received).

Creating mailing lists is the secret of success. These can be gathered from many sources. The more information you have in the data list the more effective it is likely to be.

Good Mailing Lists may be obtained from local Business Clubs, Chambers of Commerce and Local Councils.

It is also possible to purchase lists from companies such as Yellow Pages (Yell) and Thomson Directory. The best lists will have Marketing Manager/Decision Maker contact names and/or owners.

Call CT if you want more advice re: purchasing lists.

4. Referrals

A well-run magazine business will generate a high level of referred sales. If they like you and your product they will want you to do well and their contacts to benefit from the great benefits advertising in Community Times magazines offers.

When you make a sale, ask for a referral. Ask who do they know that would benefit from your magazine.

If you get a deferred sale (a sale that will happen next month or the month after), ask for a referral. People will often give you leads, as they will want your magazine to do well.

If you don't get a sale, ask for a lead or referral!

5. Follow-up

This is how you make you business work and is vital to your business.

Don't wait for someone to get back to you, in most cases they won't. It is your job to contact them!

If an owner says "leave it with me I'll call you Friday" and they don't you must call them the following week.

It shows professionalism and most importantly will bring you sales. Don't call before the agreed date it will make you come across pushy. Follow-up is important for all aspects of sales. Follow-up a face-to-face meeting with a call if required. Follow-up a telecall with a meeting, another call or a letter. Follow-up a mailshot with a call as it will increase your return five fold and lead to more meetings, more calls and most importantly increased sales and profit. Follow-up

referrals, they are your best leads. If you can, arrange a meeting. For a telephone call:

Long Term Strategy

In the first edition of your magazine you may need to suggest that advertisers take a one month advert to see what it looks like and the response they get.

The long term, recommended approach to selling advertising space is to agree fixed term agreements. These may be 3, 6, 9, or 12 month packages.

Booking space means just that, your have sold the space for that period so you know money will come in. For the advertiser it means they have agreed to pay for that space, even though they may choose to change the advert each month. Depending on what the agreement is and how much space they book they may want to negotiate a deal. Refer to the rate card and package listing for guidance.

Use your Competitive Advantage

You have numerous advantages over your competitors for your clients' advertising spend that you should take care to understand and learn how to introduce into conversations to reinforce benefits & deal with objections.

Community Times is:

A high quality, well designed glossy magazine that
will enhance your advertisers' image and brand.

An online magazine that maximizes their reach
into the local community via an online channel.

Delivered into the homes of your advertisers' prime
target market, their local community, each month and
retained.

Community Times offers advertisers the opportunity

to: Reach their local community each month via print

advertising. Attract online interest for their products

or services via the online magazine.

Attract online & offline interest via the directories.

Email the local community with product &

service offers Send SMS marketing messages

to the local community.

Your proposition to advertisers is unique. Each prospective advertiser will have existing preferred channels of marketing activity. They will also be open to new and potentially profitable channels that increase their marketing reach. As you gain experience of your local business community you will be able to "tailor" packages that best suit each customer.

CHAPTER FOUR

Produce, Publish and Distribute: Creating Value

Produce

Flat Plan (Layout Plan)

There are two main approaches to take with regard to planning your magazine layout:

Electronic

I suggest using Microsoft Publisher Master File as your Flat Plan. There are various views that you can choose depending on how you wish to manage your layout. Most people are content to use the standard layout which provides an oversized version of the selected page and links to all other pages at the bottom of the

screen.

If you are not yet comfortable with PC's or MS Publisher software using paper or a hard copy of the layout plane might be the best way to start planning your magazine.

Many experienced layout designers still like to work off hard copies so you are not alone in wanting to see your magazine on paper to plan effectively.

Paper or hard copy

Layout templates are available within the 'creating an edition' section of your Business System.

First, of course, you need to decide how many pages will be in that month's edition.

Once you have selected the appropriate layout template it is simply a matter of penciling in the pre-formatted content including editorials, articles, competitions, crosswords, su doku, Community Pages etc..

Once you have done this you can now start to add in advertisements.

You should mark these on your layout plan

separately from standard advertisements by using a different colour perhaps.

Standard advertisements are all those pages that are not premium advertisements.

As you agree advertisements with your customers you need to mark the space they have booked on the Layout Plan.

Each page may be sold as a full page, or split into variations of half pages & quarter pages.

Simply outline the appropriate space, full, half or quarter page, and write in the advertiser's name.

It will be beneficial to you to be constantly aware of what space you have available as you progress through each month. Advertisers may wish to request specific spaces and you need to ensure you don't double book space!

Before you Begin

Before you begin, read through this document and through the provided MS Publisher template.

You will require a PC running Microsoft Office 2003 and a CD or DVD writer.

Community Times (CT) will provide a monthly template which will contain the name of your Community Times magazine and contact details. On a monthly basis please save these files to your hard drive.

Open the MS Publisher document and check the information to ensure all are correct before you begin to insert the content.

Remember to save file periodically and after making

any changes. As you begin to allocate pages to

advertisers or articles, insert a text box (at least font size 36pt) and label the pages. The flat plan view can be selected by clicking: File> print preview; this will help you keep track of the magazines progress as you go along.

Your Master View Templates

Your template will contain a list of potential page-layouts depending on the requirements you can choose:

Quarter page adverts
Horizontal half page
Vertical half page

Full page
Double page spread

Editorials & Articles

On a monthly basis, your template document will include editorials and regular features, your online business system will also contain further articles. Examples of these are:

Competitions
Crosswords
Sudoku
Restaurant Reviews

Recipes

Your magazine template is based on 40 pages; you can increase as your business grows in increments of 4 pages.

Cover Page

Check the details on the cover page, e.g. the website address, date and contact details. Before inserting a cover advertisement you need to be in Master View

Master View

Master View will display the series of page layout templates provided by CT. To view these; click on View> Master page or Ctrl and **M.** Please note CT highly recommends the only master page you edit is the cover page. When in Master view the scratch area (grey area behind page) will turn yellow.

When in normal view (not in master view), to apply master page right click on the page tab at the bottom of your screen (designated by the page number). The apply master page pane will now appear. You can then select your required page layout from the drop down menu.

CT advises you work in single page spread view, but in order to check alignment> right click and choose 'view 2 page spread'.

Advertisements

There are 4 ways you could produce advertisements:

1. hrough a Freelance agent sourced yourself or through CT.

2. Direct from your client, i.e. Completed artwork provided.

3. Create the adverts yourself.

4. Use and amend a CT template.

Things to consider before producing your advertisement:

- Provide specifications and requirements,i.e. the size required, preferred format is TIFF (jpeg would be acceptable but will require re-sizing) using CMYK; Resolution 300 dpi.
- The advert sizes are as follows(in cm):
- Cover advert - 13.064 cm high x 15.4 cm wide
- Full page advert - 19.753 cm high x 14.283 cm wide
- Back cover advert – 21.6 cm high x 15.5 cm wide
- Landscape half page advert- 9.737cm high x 14.283cm wide
- Portrait half page advert - 19.753 cm high x 6.993
- Quarter page advert - 9.737 cm high x 6.968 cm wide
- Double page spread - 19.753cm high and 14.883cm wide (this includes 3mm bleed). Make sure the left page bleeds off to the right and the right page off to the left.

Content

You need to create your content on a monthly basis but

you have the flexibility to use old content and simply

update with more recent information.

Your magazine will contain statutory information also local features; editorials, etc. It's important to keep local interest with the tailored features.

Community Pages

The local information pages (community pages} are standard to the publication and should include:

- What's On

- Education

- Church & Community

- Healthcare

- Sport & Leisure

- Taxis & Takeaways (recommendations can earn revenue). This information can be collated from yellow pages, but remember to check for validity.

Now your Community Times magazine should be taking shape.

Content page

For the editor's note on the inside cover you need a photograph of yourself (don't use a holiday snap or a passport photo)

Choose 5 or 6 main features to list under contents and label with the appropriate page number.

The 'Index of advertisers' should be on the back inside cover (left page). Make a list of all your advertisers and sort into alphabetical order and note the page number the advert appears on.

New Articles

You can either copy and paste from an existing article or insert from your template document (click: insert> gallery object). I advises you use Ariel font size 9 point for general text. For general headings use Century Gothic at least size 16 to 20 dependent on space available. You should use an image for each article.

Final Checks

Proof read the whole document before burning to disk, this should be done on a single page view.

Save the Publisher document in appropriate folder. Check the size of the main monthly folder, if larger than 700MB you will need to save on more than one CD or DVD. If your file exceeds the above you can also use the publisher facility to break down into sections by clicking: file> pack and go> take to commercial printers. Label the CD with your CT reference number; name and contact number.

The monthly deadlines are located in your business system, it is imperative that the file is received by CT on or before this date, CT suggests you send by special delivery to guarantee deadlines are met.

Publish

All you need to do, whether you're arranging your own Printer, or using the Community Times service is produce a CD of your MS Publisher document for
that month's edition to the specification below.

The technical requirements are 300dpi, CYMK not RGB, necessary registration marks e.g. crop marks & at least 3mm bleed on all sides of each document.

File format PDF, all pages consolidated into single PDF

Printing

You have two options with regard to getting your magazines printed:

1. Community Times Printing Service.

We have agreements with national printers that allow us to provide our licensees with high quality, reliable & low cost printing services.

2. Your locally sourced Printing Service.

Community Times has agreements with printers who operate nationally.

Publishing online

On receipt of your CD each month CT will publish your magazine online.

Distribution

About Distribution

Distribution is, of course, key to the success of your business. Producing a fantastic looking magazine with lots of great content is meaningless if it isn't delivered to your community on time and effectively each month.

You have a contract with your advertisers &
Community Times that states you will
ensure delivery of a minimum of 3,500
magazines
to your community each month.

A lot of people enjoy the physical activity
involved in delivering magazines and only
feel reassured that deliveries are happening
if they are personally involved.

Our perspective is that the time you devote
to your business should be a cost effective
as possible. Whether you operate your
business around family, work or other
commitments your time is your most
valuable commodity.

Distribution can be purchased cheaply and

will
free up not only the time taken to actually
distribute the magazine but also the time
taken up with organizing and managing
activity.

There is a strong commercial case to
contract out distribution as the time you
save can be utilized on more productive

and profitable areas of your business.

Self Distribution

Lots of new licensees start their business with the intention of distributing their magazines themselves with the help of friends & family.

It is quite common after one or two editions that friends & family start falling foul of mystery ailments towards the end of each month!

The serious point is that distribution of your magazine is a serious undertaking & relying on goodwill is not the most sensible method of ensuring effective delivery.

At the least you should make sure that your distributors are rewarded appropriately and will be available when required, even if it's cold & raining.

Each person should be capable of delivering

50 magazines per hour. This means that delivery of 3,500 magazines will take 70 man hours i.e. 70 people 1 hour, 35 people 2 hours, 5 people 14 hours etc..

If you are able to organise this activity effectively & reliably it can provide useful pocket money for nieces & nephews.

Remember safety is paramount and you have a duty of care to your distributors to ensure they are well briefed, safe & organised.

The Royal Mail offers a door to door distribution service. The service is offered by a specialist department within Royal Mail, Door to Door.

A 40 page magazine weighs approximately 62g. Costs are c£76 per thousand to deliver to postcode sectors. There is, however, a minimum charge of £500.

To find out more visit, www.royalmail.com

Others

Almost every region has specialist distribution companies who provide door to door delivery solutions to a wide variety of companies and deal with many varieties of printed material.

These companies are often cheaper than Royal Mail as they do not provide a UK wide service & utilize their specialist local knowledge and workforce.

It is likely that you will require a "Salus" distribution. This means that your magazine is not delivered with a variety of other leaflets or as an insert but is pushed through letterboxes as an individual item. This is the best form of delivery for your magazine & will most likely be the preferred option of your distributors.

To find out contact details of distribution companies in your region simply email or call us.

CHAPTER FIVE

Getting Started, Prepare to Succeed

Setting up your office

Stationery

Bank Account

Your Business System

Setting up your office

Setting up your office doesn't mean you need a bespoke, solid oak, fitted home office with cutting edge technology . You would be wise to minimise costs at this stage and wiser still to continue with this philosophy as your business grows. Keeping costs low is one of the keys to all successful businesses.

Your home office can be anywhere in the house where you can set up a desk for your PC with an Internet connection, make & receive phone calls and have room to store your files.

There are, of course, a few items of technology that will prove invaluable in running an efficient business. First the essentials;

PC

The key application software that you need to run is Microsoft Office. This means you don't require a top of the range, specialist computer.

Most PC's arrive with MS Publisher already installed on the machine. If you have to purchase the software you should expect to pay c£100.

Your package includes all of the URL's & email addresses you need to operate your business.

INTERNET CONNECTION

You will be able to manage your business with a dial-up connection but would benefit greatly from a broadband connection as you will be sending and receiving graphic files which can be large and may therefore take a considerable time to download through a dialup connection. A further advantage of broadband is that you will be able to use the same phone line for incoming and outgoing calls at the same time as being online.

For up to date recommendations from our technical team email us from your ct:manage system or call 01792 773399

PRINTER

A colour printer is a necessity as you will be creating proofs for approval by your advertisers. The major cost implication to consider is the price of ink cartridge replacements as this can prove expensive.

SCANNER

This is another necessity as many advertisers will have printed material which they will wish you to use for their advertisements.

FAX

The ability to send & receive faxes is essential. A number of customers will use faxes to send information to you & may require faxed documents from you.

Efax or a similar service should be a consideration if you don't wish to clutter up your working area with a fax machine.

PS: If space is a constraint you might want to consider an all in one scanner, fax & printer.

TELEPHONE

You will need a telephone and we recommend a billing system that allows you to make local calls cheaply. An answer service is a good investment as prospective advertisers will not be impressed if their calls go unanswered and they are unable to leave a message. If start-up funds allow we would recommend a hands- free phone that allows you to write & operate a keyboard whilst holding a phone conversation.

DIGITAL CAMERA

Many advertisers will want you to take photographs of them, their staff, their shops or specific products. Photographs of restaurant owners and their staff are particularly popular alongside your review.

Other items that may be worth considering are:

LAPTOP

Whilst a little more expensive than a desktop PC, a laptop provides you with increased flexibility and a portable PC that you can use to demonstrate your online offerings to prospective advertisers. A GPRS card will enable you to connect with the Internet and give prospective advertisers a full demonstration of your services.

Nowadays lots of communal areas have wireless Internet networks available, e.g. McDonald's restaurants in the UK all have connections available.

Many licensees also find the flexibility provided by a laptop useful if they find themselves away from their home office with time on their hands. Your ct:manage business system is accessible via an Internet connection which will enable you to manage your business from any location that affords web access.

STATIONERY

Professional stationery will go a long way to re-assuring advertisers that your new business is a professional and well run operation.

Your Community Times magazine is a high quality product and this impression should be reinforced to your prospective advertisers with well designed and good quality business stationery.

Our designers have produced designs to which you simply need to add your personal details and send to a printer. The key items as you will see from the design templates are:

- Business Cards
- Compliment Slips
- Headed Paper

If you would like us to organise printing of business stationery simply email or call and we will arrange for your personalised stationery to be printed & delivered to you. Prices vary and will be available before order confirmation.

BANK ACCOUNT

Cashflow is always a critical issue for business success. Even seemingly successful businesses can fail because they run out of cash.

Your Community Times business offers you a significant commercial advantage as you will be collecting cash in advance of paying for the printing services you require. This means you should always run a cash positive business.

A separate bank account will help you to easily identify and account for every item of income & expenditure.

Credibility is also an issue. Community Times magazines are a high quality, well designed marketing channel that will attract advertising spend from small and large businesses. Presenting an invoice to a large, established company that is payable to your personal account presents the wrong image of your business.

Many of your clients will allocate an increasing proportion of their annual advertising spend to you and it is important to establish effective long-term relationships at the outset.

DSL Accounting, the award winning DSA member firm, have developed a bespoke cash accounting system for Community Times licensees to manage their business effectively and tax efficiently.

ABOUT THE AUTHOR

Joshua Aondoakaa was the Editor-in-Chief of the Heathrow Community Times. A local airport community magazine delivered free to homes and businesses around the Heathrow Airport area. After a very successful and rewarding career as Editor of the widely read community magazine, Joshua ran his own local free magazine successfully in the West London area for many years. Delivering to local homes, business and corporate offices. During this time he has developed extensive knowledge and expertise in free community magazine start-ups and has written this book to help those who have passion for starting their own successful community magazine. You will find in the pages of the book most valuable information that will give you thumbs up to start your won free community magazine in no time.